Life is not a Dance Rehearsal

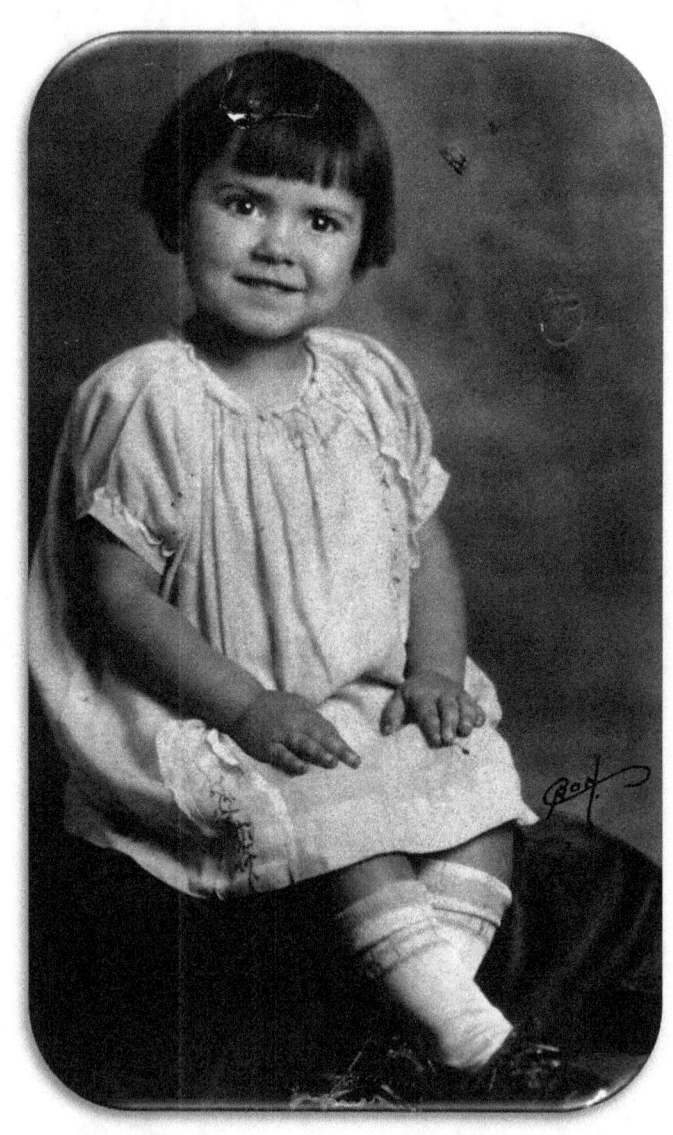

Memories of My Life

To My Editor

I thank you, my April, for all the long hours of assisting me with the history of each era, putting this together. We have had a lot of fun and laughs commiserating about it all. We did it. We got there, and I thank you so much for everything. I love you forever and always. Mom.

My Children

My thanks to everyone for all the encouragement you have given me to continue and to finish writing this book. Nick Seitz for teaching me how to use my iPad to put this on the computer, email and print. Denise, for remembering and reminding me of some dates. Mike Murphy for printing the first draft. Stacy for helping to look for and choose a cover for our book. It all came together at last thanks to all.

To my Husband

This book could not have been printed without the help and support of my husband. Jerry has helped me in so many ways, fixing the computer, remembering a name, or mostly just giving me lots of encouragement. Thank you my darling Pittsburg. You know I love you forever, Your Chicken Flower.

To my Grandchildren

Life is not a race, but indeed a journey to enjoy.

Be honest, work hard, be choosy, say thank you, I love you, and great job to someone each day.

Let your handshake mean more than pen and paper. Stand tall, be positive, look direct, with a smile.

Dreaming does matter. It allows us to become that which you aspire to be.

Appreciate the little things in life and enjoy them. Some of the best things really are free.

Do not worry about the small stuff, and try always to give more than you get. Take time for yourself.

PLAN FOR LONGEVITY

Prologue

When you start to think of what you have and what you have not said, what you have done and what you have not done, there are also many times you wish could have been different, but reflecting doesn't help. It's just what it is.

I feel very blessed that God has given me a life of more ups than downs. Everyone chooses a path to follow and can decide what to do. This story of my life is what I choose to do. So much left unsaid, and so much left undone…

Life is Not a Dance Rehearsal

By Darlene Seitz

Copyright © 2014 by Darlene Seitz

Seitz, Darlene

All Rights Reserved. No part of this book may be reproduced, stored in a retrieval system, or transmitted in any form or by any means, electronic, mechanical, photocopying, recording, or otherwise, without permission in writing from Michael Ray King Publishing, Inc.

Michael Ray King Publishing

PO Box 33431

Palm Coast FL 32135

www.ClearViewPressInc.com

Printed in the United States of America

Table of Contents

1920's	Roaring 20's	1
1930's	Depression	3
1940's	World War II	11
1950's	My Plane	21
1960's	Jerry	44
1970's	Grandchildren	54
1980's	Future Abrasives	59
1990's	Sammy	63
2000's	Golf	65
2010's	Retirement	72

1920's

Mildred Darlene Colclasure was born July 2nd, 1925 and the world was a much different place from where I sit now writing on my computer, nearly nine decades later. My mother, Margaret Irene Miller and father, Cletus Colclasure lived in Kankakee, Illinois on a rented farm. Mother was one of eleven children and was raised in Springfield, Illinois. My mother's siblings were Edith, Sherill, Jaunita, Caroline, Jessie, Laurence, Mildred, Lillian, Margaret and Sonia. I was named Darlene Mildred after my aunt Mildred who was nicknamed Mickey. The night I was born, mom said she sat up in bed and my Aunt Edith caught me in a blanket as I came out screaming. It was not long after that Mom and Edith took me back to Springfield, where we lived with Grandma Miller. Mom then divorced my father.

We lived in Springfield, Illinois with Grandmother Miller until I was 4 years old. I can still remember sitting on grandma Millers comfortable lap and eating the warm bread she made and fed me with milk and honey in front of the wood stove with the cat curled up behind it.

Mother and I then moved to Southside Chicago and lived with Aunt Juanita who had 2 children, my cousins, Eleanor and Bill Colandra. We next moved to share an apartment with Aunt Jesse who had a daughter, my cousin, Ellen Jackson, who was my age. Ellen and I had a lot of fun together. One day we decided to walk to the movie theater, King Kong was playing but we didn't have any money for a ticket so we asked if we could use the bathroom, the man just smiled and let us in. The movie was so exciting and scary that I didn't want to get up to use the bathroom when I really had to go. When the movie was over the line for the bathroom was so long that I couldn't wait and I just peed my pants. I was so embarrassed and my long stockings showed the wet so I asked Ellen to walk behind me, she said No, but did walk behind me all the way home. We really got heck from our moms, they were worried we were lost.

In the year I was born, Calvin Coolidge was President, the first Sears store opened in Chicago, Scotch tape was invented and a school teacher was charged in Tennessee for teaching the theory of evolution to school children. The decade of 1920's was best known as the Roaring 20's, so called for its excess and opulence. Following the end of World War 1, people were able to buy homes and jobs were plentiful. Technology and invention resumed and the radio came on the scene, quickly becoming a must have means of entertainment and news for families. Airplanes began the delivery of out of town mail. Baseball was America's favorite pastime as Babe Ruth and The Yankees set world records. The consumption and sale of alcohol was prohibited in 1919 which led to the rise of gangsters in America, the most notorious being Al Capone. The Charleston was the popular dance and the music of Duke Ellington and Al Jolson was all the rage. This was also the decade that Henry Ford introduced the Model-T car, forever changing our mode of transportation. The fun and opulence of the 1920's continued until that fateful day, October 24th, 1929, known as Black Thursday when the stock market crashed and started The Great Depression.

1930's

The economy had collapsed and people lost their life savings, their homes and their jobs. President Herbert Hoover, who took office in 1929, the year of the crash, was blamed for the country's decline and was replaced by Fraklin D. Roosevelt in 1933. President Roosevelt was a popular President who encouraged the people and was the only President to remain in office for three terms.

Families who lost their jobs and homes due to the economic collapse were moving to the streets and Shantytowns were formed. Shantytowns were literally towns of people who created shelter and hovels out of wood and cardboard and were provided heat by community campfires. As these Shantytowns, also referred to as Homverville's after the sitting President Hoover, sprang up across America. Food was rationed and jobs were few, creating long lines for both food and any menial jobs being offered. Some people out of desperation began lives of crime and some such as the famous bank robbers Bonnie and Clyde were celebrated for their two-year rampage of robbing banks until they were gunned down and killed in 1934.

The city dwellers were not the only ones affected by the depression as the Great Plains region fell into destruction following an eight-year drought. This drought as well as poor farming techniques used by farmers created what came to be know as The Dust Bowl. The land became useless to farm and uninhabitable to live due to black storms of dust that swirled the land. This caused thousands of farmers to abandon their homes and livelihood in search of any work to survive. Many hitched a ride on a ral car headed to California where conditions were said to be good for farming.

The 1930's also saw the rise of Hitler's Third Reich and the first concentration camp 'Dachau' was opened in 1933 shortly after Hitler became Chancellor of Germany. This atrocity called Holocaust continued for many years to come with many more concentration camps and an untold number of lives lost. It wasn't until 1945 at the end of World War II that prisoners who had survived this hell were liberated.

As baseball continued to be America's favorite pastime, Joe DiMaggio, playing for the New York Yankees becomes a new baseball superstar.

In 1931, The Empire State Building sprang up in New York and became a travel destination and a wonder to be seen.

When we entered into the 1930's and I had celebrated my 5th Birthday, Mother took me back to Kankakee Illinois to spend time with my Dad and Grandma and Grandpa Benner. She needed to work and Chicago at that time was not a good place for a child with all the unrest of the depression.

I lived with my grandparents in a farm house with a large kitchen, two bedrooms and a living area. The screened porch had a horse trough filled with water and a pump to pour our water from. There was also a butter churn on the porch and we enjoyed fresh biscuits Grandma Benner made with warm churned butter and fresh canned jam. Grandma was busy all the time. She made our clothes on her sewing machine while always singing and laughing all the while. She also made me dolls that I loved. We had a barn with cows, pigs and horses and a huge garden. It was fun to milk the cows and squirt milk at the cats. After a long day of work on the farm Grandpa Benner would sit in the Rocker on the porch and I would crawl up on his lap and rub his old bald head.

My Aunt Edith, my mother's oldest sister who was there at my birth, still lived in Kankakee about a mile from the Benner's farm. Aunt Edith and Uncle Wes had three children, my cousins, Sherell, Juanita and Larry. One day, we were playing at their house and I broke a lamp, Aunt Edith scolded me and sent me home. I had ridden my pony Pal over to the house as was my habit however when I was sent home I was crying so hard and was so upset that I got turned around and frightened that I was lost. I started crying out for help, I heard my name called and thought it was God but it turned out to be my cousin Sherrill who lead me home safely.

Once, at Edith and Wes' house, during a bad thunder storm, a horse standing under a tree in a storm was struck by lightning and died. Grandpa then skinned the horse for the leather. It was fun for us kids jumping on a skin trampoline.

I remember a time too when Aunt Edith went out to slop the hogs but her dog had opened the gate to the pen and a big sow grabbed Edith and threw her down in the pen. Luckily, her dog jumped over the fence and staved off the sow while she got out. Aunt Edith was mauled, but it never stopped her from doing her chores.

I have many memories of my time on that farm and had mixed feeling on leaving, happy to get back with my mom in Chicago and sad to leave the relationships I had formed on the farm. I loved Grandma Benner and the happiness she brought to the home. I learned later that she had always kept my dolls for me but I never saw her again. Aunt Edith later moved to Springfield, Illinois where she became a teacher and lived in her home at 2412 Lowell Ave. where she lived to be 103.

The Trip to Oregon

On returning to Chicago to be with my mother, I learned that while I had been away, Mom had met and fallen in love with Jerry Nott who was to become my stepfather. It was decided with conditions so bad in Chicago that we, Mom, Jerry and I would move west to Oregon. Jerry had been in the Marines with a friend named Foote and he had told Jerry how beautiful Oregon was and how plentiful the jobs were.

Chicago with cousins - 8 years old

When we left Chicago, I remember there being riots in the streets, people throwing milk cans and long lines standing and waiting for any food available. We left in a small black car that I never thought would make it but we were on our way to what we pictured as paradise. We drove and drove, slept in the car and ate whenever we could. It was fun seeing all the sights and wildlife along the way. I saw deer, fox and bear but was not afraid of them, I tried to seek them out in the woods any time we stopped. One place we went through in Wyoming was called 'Old Faithful' and was a geyser shooting hot water high up in the air. Another wonder we saw was Mt. Rushmore the Presidents faces carved in stone on the side of a high mountain. It was miraculous to me that the artist could climb so high to put those faces on the mountain.

We also stopped along the way at Aunt Kit's small hut on the side of a mountain in Montana. I wasn't sure who she was but she was a nice old lady with a big bear of a dog. I made the mistake of pretending deer antlers on my head and woofing at the dog, it charged and jumped on me but thankfully Mom grabbed me and Aunt Kit whistled for the dog to release me. Since then I have had a greater respect and caution of animals. While in Montana, Dad (as I now called my stepfather Jerry) did some stream panning for gold. He was lucky in finding a few nuggets so we cashed them in and got on our way.

In Washington, the apple picking time was prime and Mom and Dad were hired to pick apples and were happy to replenish our funds. They placed me in a one room, all grades school house while they picked. I was in what would have been second grade then and I didn't know much but the teacher had a ruler and made sure everyone paid attention. The other children were browner than me and I couldn't understand them. They were from Mexico and probably thought I was from outer space.

When the apple picking season was over we were back on our way to Oregon to find Dads friend Foote.

As we arrived in Oregon along the Columbia River, looking at all the tall green trees and flowers, we just knew we were in God's country. Wow, there was snowcapped Mt. Hood overlooking all of Portland, we have reached our final destination, almost. We just needed to find Dads friend Foote. Foote had told Dad he lived in Oregon City just outside Portland. We were so excited to meet them after traveling for so long all across the country. We finally found the address Foote had given Dad and at last arrived in their driveway. Though we are anxious to get out, Dad asked us to wait in the car while he went to the door. Dad was greeted at the door by Foote who said, "Hello and I'm sorry but you can't come in, my wife won't allow it". My Dad was so taken back he said, "well let's just have a cup of coffee and catch up", to which Foote replied," No, I can't and you need to leave now". So, with much disappointment, let down, hungry and tears in our eyes we left and drove to a small town nearby called Sellwood. The next day Dad found a house to paint. The lady whose house it was said we could stay in her guest house out back while Dad was painting her house and she gave us some food and some money. It seems as though no matter how bad things get, somehow God steps in and turns things around.

We lived in a small place in Sellwood for about a year and I went to school. I was nine then and went into 3rd grade in school. Though I had never really completed 1st or 2nd grade, I had memorized the times tables and alphabet and with a lot of help at home made it to the 4th grade.

Following our time and Dad's work in Sellwood, we bought a home for a total of $1000 in Milwaukie about 5 miles from Sellwood. We had walked back and forth about ten miles several times while looking. The home was wonderful, it had a kitchen, 2 bedrooms, a living room and a bath. The address was 1926 4th Ave., Milwaukie, Oregon. Mom and Dad worked very hard to fix it up. We had a vegetable garden, chickens and rabbits. Dad also went hunting so we had plenty to eat and Mom canned vegetables and fruit. Mom taught me to sew and as I completed grade school and into Jr. High, I made most of my clothes.

I could take the school bus to school but by the time I was in High School, I liked to walk. This entailed crossing the Interstate Highway and over a footbridge over a lake and about a mile on. There was a train trestle behind our house and I figured out I could avoid the highway and lake by going that way so I took the chance several times. There is no way to get off it if a train came so it was very dangerous. I learned of a boy I knew from school getting run over by the train, still this did not stop me from many times hitching a ride on the trains caboose and riding it down to the logging dump.

The logging dump was a large open slide where the train dumped the large tree logs into the Willamette River. The logs were then pushed together into a raft and tied so a tug boat could pull them to the mill where they were cut up into lumber. This was really interesting to watch.

In the summer months, I enjoyed swimming in the river just a block from our house. But the most fun though was dancing when my parents took me with them to the dancehall on

Saturday night. After dancing for a while I would get tired and go to sleep on a bench until it was time to go home.

If the 1920's had been a time of abundance and folly, the 1930's had been a time of hardship and despair. The stock market and economy had collapsed and many people lost their life savings, their homes and their jobs. President Herbert Hoover, who took office in 1929, the year of the crash, was blamed for the country's decline and was replaced by Franklin D. Roosevelt in 1933. President Roosevelt was a popular President who encouraged the people and was the only President to remain in office for 3 terms.

One of the best things to come out of the 1930's was The Big Band and Swing Era which included Duke Ellington, Tommy Dorsey and Benny Goodman, to name just a few. I remember going to a dance hall every Saturday night, the music and dancing kept our spirits up during the Great Depression and World War II.

1940's

The 1930's had passed and we had entered the 1940's. The 1940's were dominated by World War II. The first ever use of the nuclear bomb was used on Hiroshima and Nagasaki following the bombing of Pearl Harbor in Hawaii. For the first time ever, single women were recruited as well as men to serve their country. Women served the military in ranks of WASP's, WAVE's and nurses. On the home front for the first time, women and blacks were allowed to take jobs previously only held by white males. Rosie the Riveter became on of the many famous icons for the era.

Resources of food and other everyday necessities became tight due to limited distribution and production and rationing began in 1943. War Bonds were issued and became popular as a means to support the war. A person could buy a bond and redeem it ten years later for a guaranteed return value. With the country all working together, the war time production of weaponry and supplies needed to support our troops pulled our country out of the Great Depression.

It was 1945 before World War II ended and out troops began returning home victorious. On returning home, Bets who had come from farms initially were now setting up home closer to the city and suburbs were formed. Women who had served or worked now knew an independence they hadn't know before.

Blacks who had served in the military or worked for wages were no longer willing to accept a lesser status though it would be some time yet before their voices were heard. World War II led to many changes yet to come from previous American life.

Baseball resumed as the most popular sport following the war and Jackie Robinson, the first black man to play professional sports was signed by the Brooklyn Dodgers and became the new baseball great.

Sometime around my 13th year my mother received a letter from her sister, my Aunt Lillian, in Springfield, Illinois, that my Grandmother was dying and wanted all of her children with her. We didn't have the money to go but Mom said that we were going no matter what or how. So, Mom and I set out by bus but ended up hitching rides with car and trucks along the way. I remember at one point sleeping under a tree and in barns but don't remember much else other than arriving at Grandma's house before she died. We stayed in Illinois until I graduated from the 8th grade. I lived with my Aunt Carrie, Uncle Ollie and my cousins, Sis, Bob and Alfred. We always went to church and I memorized the Ten Commandments and was given a copy of the bible. While we were there, I decided to visit my father, Cletus Colclasure who lived on a farm outside of Springfield. I had not seen or spoke with him in years but remembered the same handsome smile when I saw him. He was now married to a school teacher and had 3 children of their own. I enjoyed staying a day and never saw them again until his funeral years later.

Mother and I returned to Oregon and it was around this time that Dad brought his mother, Jenny Nott, his father Charles Nott, his brother Charles Nott and his brother's wife and 18 year old daughter out to live in Oregon. His brother Warren had gotten a job with the fire department in Milwaukie but sadly died trying to rescue a girl who had run her car into a lake. He was declared a hero and a statue was erected in Milwaukie in his memory.

Oh, how I loved to roller skate, Oaks Park was across the river from us and had a big roller rink. It was great fun to whirl around the floor, listening to the loud organ music. It took a while, but I learned to dance on skates and this was my heaven, making up steps to the music as I skated. I guess this is where my love for dancing started and eventually led to my career with Arthur Murray Dance Studio. I remember one night sneaking out the window to go to the rink at Oaks Park with my friends because my parents did not allow me to go out at night.

I was not a good school student and didn't really like school but I really enjoyed the social activities. I was the lead in two school plays and was a cheerleader until I couldn't afford to buy the sweater. We used to dance at lunch in the cafeteria until I got a job at the ice cream shop called Diane's. I started spending my lunches working there at noon and after school. My pay to start was .25 cents an hour. I enjoyed working and was 15 years old. I was still in school at the start of the 1940's and went to the dancehall every Saturday night with my girlfriend Nina Maxwell. We loved to dance to the music of Glen Miller and all the greats.

I met my first great love at the dancehall. His name was Jack Brown and he had graduated from Franklin high school and had attended one year at the University of Oregon. We danced and he gave me a ride home that first night we met and asked if he could call me the next day. I had plans to go skiing up on Mt.

Hood the next day but said that he could call later. When he called the next day my Dad told him, "You can't see her now, she broke her leg skiing." Well, he was over at my house within a half hour. I had a big cast on my leg so Jack took me to the dance the following Saturday to have everyone sign it. From that time on we were together and so much in love.

While I was in typing class, December 7th, 1941, that an announcement came over the loud speaker at school that Japan had attacked Pearl Harbor and we were at war. Everyone was stunned and afraid because there were rumors that Japan would move on to also attack the west coast where we lived. It was an unbelievable and frightening time. While I was at work later, my Japanese friend, Art Yo Shawl came in to tell me goodbye. He said that his family, as well as many Japanese families were being sent to Internment camps in California. I was so sad and felt it was unfair he was being punished for something that he and his family didn't do. He and his family were Americans just like me. But this was war.

Following the announcement of war, Jack said he wanted to join the military and fight for his country so we decided to get married first so we could be together longer.

Lieutenant Jack Brown

Jack and I were married on December 12, 1942. We had a beautiful wedding in a small historical church with his friend Pat as best man and my friend Nina as maid of honor. The reception was at our home in Milwaukie and Mom fixed everything. All of our friends were there and we had a wonderful time.

Our time together continued until Jack joined the Air force to become a fighter pilot and was shipped out to San Antonio, Texas to earn his wings. He wrote to me every day while he was in training telling me he missed me and I wrote him telling him everything that was going on at home. We couldn't call each other because any communication there was at that time were reserved for the military use. I had taken a job as a riveter in the same factory as Mom and later came to work in the office. I was not so good with typing so I mostly did filing and showed important visitors around the factory. One day we had a film star visit and all I could think to say to him was Wow, you sure have big feet. My job there didn't last too long probably because I filed everything under C or P. C for correspondence and P for paper, it made sense to me.

Since Jack was still in his basic training, I headed by bus to San Antonio. At that time wife's were not allowed to stay with their husbands and were not given any allotments but I didn't care because I was closer to Jack. I stayed at the YWCA for free and I had to fib about being married to a service man to get a job at a drugstore because their policy was to not hire short term help. One hot Texas day I went swimming at a public pool and when I got out discovered that someone had stolen my shoes. I rode the bus back barefoot and blistered from walking on the burning pavement. I became aware that all the black people rode in the back of the bus. I knew blacks were not allowed in most restaurants or to drink from public drinking fountains. I think it was Rosa Parks, the first black women to refuse a seat in the back of the bus that helped change history for black people.

Picture of Jack's training plane

I didn't get to see Jack a lot during his training but I was there for his graduation when he got his wings. He was then sent to a base in Lincoln, Nebraska where we were able to live together. I was 8 months pregnant with who was soon to become our son 'Jackie' when Jack left on his last training mission.

Gladys, Jacks mother was there visiting with us in anticipation of the birth of her grandchild. Jack and 36 other pilots were up on what was supposed to be their last training mission prior to shipping oversees when lightning struck their plane, bringing the plane down and killing all aboard. I thought I saw Jacks face before me that night, smiling and walking up the steps of our home with his hat in his hand. The next morning, two officers came to the door to give us the news. I was shocked and devastated but still felt him with me. It seemed his arms were around me. I thought about how he had explained a few nights earlier that he might be killed and what to do. He must have had a premonition.

When I called my mother she got worried and set off driving to Nebraska with Gramps, Jacks stepdad and Gladys husband.

Wives of pilots killed in storm

Meanwhile, because of my condition, the Air Force had

arranged to fly me home. Gladys, who had just lost her son and was also devastated, stayed in Nebraska to await the arrival of my mother and Gramps and drove back with them. When I arrived alone and beyond grief back in Portland, I called my friend Nina to pick me up. We went to our friend Martha's house where I went into labor and was taken to the hospital to deliver Jackie on August 10th, 1944, just one week following losing Jack on August 3rd, 1944.

I was not able to attend Jacks funeral as I was still in the hospital with Jackie so an Air Force Officer came to the hospital and presented me with the folded American Flag. I felt so totally lost and sad. The flag made it real. He was killed – that's when I started to cry a lot, but I knew Jack had left me with the greatest gift in the world, his son and Jackie became my world.

Though Jackie had been born premature and weighed only 5 lbs., 6 oz., he soon caught up to become a happy and healthy baby. After mother returned from Nebraska with Gladys and Gramps, she took me and Jackie home. She was wonderful, she had decorated a crib and high chair and all our friends and family came by to welcome us home, offer condolences and celebrate Jackie's birth. It was an odd combination. In the days that followed, as much as I loved Jackie I was still crying and grieving over my loss of Jack. When I lost so much weight (89 pounds) that I couldn't breast feed Jackie and he also started crying all the time, we started formula. I knew it was time to snap out of it. Mom started buying me milkshakes to drink. I started leaving the house with Jackie, taking him to the swimming pool and friend's houses with me. This seemed to do the trick and I became more myself again.

The war was still going and I became aware that the sacrifices of other peoples love ones to the war were all around me. During my time away, my friend Nina had married and her husband who was also a bomber pilot had been shot down over Germany and taken prisoner. I was glad to be with her during her time of need. He was fortunately released and returned to Nina after the war ended in 1945.

The war had really united our country and brought everyone together working toward a common goal. We all sang patriotic songs together proudly, and gladly endured the rations of food, sugar, coffee and gas. We were all jubilant to have won the war and have our soldiers come home but also sad for the Japanese to have had to resort to such devastating measures. We had really only heard rumors through the war of Hitler and his horrible concentration camps and it wasn't until after the war and the liberation of the prisoners that we knew the extent of it.

Baseball continued to be a favorite pastime and Joe DiMaggio, playing for The New York Yankees became the new baseball superstar. The Empire State Building sprang up in New York and became a wonder to be seen. It was also in the 30's that we were all panicked by Orson Wells "War of The Worlds" radio broadcast declaring the Martians were landing on earth until we were told it was just a fictional radio show.

After we entered the 1940's and the war broke out, life changed for my family, as it had for every American. Dad joined up with the Merchant Mariners and Mom took a job as a riveter in a factory making aircraft parts. Merchant Mariners were made up of men from all walks of life that had a desire to serve their country. They were assigned to 'Liberty Ships' and sailed the

World as was needed to provide supplies to our soldiers. Many of the ships were bombed by the Germans and many brave men lost their lives serving their country on these ships.

My step father, Jerry Nott, joined the Merchant Marines and was stationed on a ship with the Matson Line. He started as a basic seaman. He studied to work his way up to first mate before he retired at the end of the war. The many stories he had to tell about his adventures were amazing. One I remember so well was while he was away for a very long time, mother was so worried that he may have died because we never got any news about him. One day, he finally came home and said that his ship was bombed by the Germans and sunk off the coast of Africa. All the crew were in the ocean. Some made it, others not, but he was lucky enough to get into a life boat. They were picked up after several days at sea.

1950's

I worked as a waitress in a bar during the last year of the war and made good money in tips from the service men and could spend my days with Jackie. It was during this time, a friend of mine said he was going to take flying lessons at The Scappoose airfield. I remembered how Jack had told me how wonderful it was to fly, like being close to God and so I signed up for lessons also. I loved every minute of it. We started out in a small Aronca plane and it took me about eight flights before I could solo. I felt like I was sharing something with Jack and was never afraid as I knew I had his hand on my shoulder.

My plane PT-19 Fairchild Army Trainer

When I heard they were selling used Army trainer planes I could have reconditioned and licensed, I put my car up at the bank and with the money I was saving from waitressing, bought a plane. It had two open cockpits, low wings and I painted it silver with a red stripe down the side. I eventually began work at the airfield and rented my plane out for $25.00 an hour as I continued flying lessons and paid for my plane's storage and gas.

While working there at the airfield, I learned to play bridge. Jackie was about 2 years old by then and I took him to work with me where he loved to run around and everyone knew him. I loved to fly my plane and had several adventures. I practiced touch down landings and it was a good thing I had. Once I flew with the Breakfast Club, down to Oceanside Beach, where the mayor came out to meet us. It was a fun group to fly with. Another time, when Dad's ship The Mattson was in port on the Columbia River, I flew over it and did pylon eights. I could see Dad waving his arms at me probably hoping I wouldn't crash onto his ship.

One of Jacks friends, who were attending the University of Oregon, invited me down for his graduation so I flew my plane down to Eugene. While there, I stayed in the girls Sorority dorm and went to the dance. That night the boys serenaded us in the dorm. One of the guys asked if he could hitch a ride back with me but I didn't check to make sure there was enough oil and gas in the plane. It was somewhere over Milwaukie that the plane started to sputter. I decided to land and picked out a field with a cow in the middle of it. I flew over the trees, banked left and as we came down landing hard, we bumped over the cow. My poor passenger was so relieved to land, he kissed the ground once he got out of the plane.

My last adventure though was the end of my plane and almost of me, I was flying to Milwaukie to go to Moms house and was planning to land on a strip that a friend was fixing up for his plane. I flew over the strip and turned a hard left over a steep bank obscuring my vision of what was below, I was caught in a strong wind so I dipped my left wing and didn't see the gas tanks (no gas in them yet) sitting on the logs on the right side, my right wing hit them and the plane ground looped. This time I kissed the ground after they dug me out, leaving me with only the propeller (which our Son Steve still has) and my memories of my fun flying adventures.

Bob & I and our mothers in backyard wedding

Arthur Murray Dance Studios

It was time to move on, to find a job. Since I loved dancing, I decided to apply and trained to become a dance instructor. The training to learn all six dances too four weeks, then memorize the sales manual that Katherine Murray wrote. After much practice, I discovered my niche with the studio as I had a natural ability for dance, for teaching, and for sales.

Dinner with Katherine Murray in New York

It was at the Portland studio that I met and married Robert Newberry who was also an instructor at the Portland studio. We were married, June 6th 1948 in a back yard wedding at Moms house with our friends and family in attendance.

Shortly after that we were sent to Boise, Idaho to open a studio owned by Peg and Steve Boyton. However, we soon received a surprise when Bob was recalled back to Camp Pendleton in San Diego, by the Marines to serve an additional year during the Korean War. Bob had been a tank commander with the Marines in World War 11 and had already served and been released, however, they were able to recall him during the Korean War. During this year, while Bob served, Jackie and I lived in San Diego. We lived in a boarding home near Bob's base and I worked part time at the Studio in San Diego. Jackie was watched by a woman who also had a room in the same house while I worked. We spent our weekends visiting the zoo, the ports and seeing the sights in San Diego.

Dwight D. Eisenhower was nominated President in 1953 and remained in office for two terms to 1961.

The Cold War came to be in the 50's. A standoff of sorts, as a result of the Soviet East and the Capitalist West both having the power and technology for a nuclear holocaust. Fortunately both sides realized this was not the answer.

The 1950's also introduced the Rock and Roll Era when radios began playing the music of what was to become the Rock & Roll greats of Elvis Presley, Jerry Lee Lewis and Buddy Holly. Following Elvis airing on the Ed Sullivan Show in 1958, he became known as the King of Rock & Roll. This was also the era of the famous crooners like Frank Sinatra, Perry Como and Nat King Cole.

Diners also sprang up and became popular places for young people to meet and enjoy jukebox music, mingle with friends and eat burgers and shakes.

Televisions were now the must have for entertainment in family homes and in 1951, color was added and sitcoms such as I love Lucy, The Honeymooners and Lassie became popular. Soap Operas were also introduced and became a huge means of advertisement on television to sell their products to housewives of America.

Baseball continues and the New York teams, the Yankees, the Giants and the Dodgers rule the 1950's.

Disneyland is opened by Walt Disney in 1955 and becomes the coveted travel destination by old and young alike.

The start of equality laws were taking a stand when it was decided that education for blacks was to remain separate but equal. One of the first big changes for equality.

By the time Bob, Jackie and I returned back to Portland, we had entered into the 1950's. It was the early part of 1951 that Bob and I learned we were pregnant with who was to become our darling daughter. Denise Susan Newberry was born December 16th 1951 in Portland, Oregon. We couldn't have been happier than to have our chubby and adorable little girl.

Following our return to Portland, Bob and I resumed working at the Portland studio. During the next years, Jackie and Denise spent a great deal of time with Gladys and Gramps while Bob and I were working at the studio.

Gramps was a Modoc Indian. He was married to Gladys Crim, Jack's mother. He was not relation to Jack, but a very

5 Point buck I shot at Klannath Falls

good fatherly influence. They spent time in the summer months at the reservation in Klamath Falls, Oregon. Jackie, Denise and I enjoyed occasionally going with them. It was great fun to sleep in a tent, cook on a campfire, swim in the river and hunt from the back of a pickup truck.

While we were hunting one day with the old Indian that rode in the back with me, I bagged my first deer. The old Indian told the story thereafter of the black haired she devil with long red nails who was just like a "big black cat" shooting the 5 pointer buck from the back of the truck. It is an Indian tradition that after the kill, the buck is dressed out, and a bite is taken of the liver. This shows appreciation for the food the animal provides. I still have that buck's horns in our garage.

Another time on the reservation, I went duck hunting down the river and shot a duck which I had to swim out in the freezing water to retrieve. I held the duck by its feet while I walked back to camp. I kept hearing the bushes rustle and the hair on the back of my neck started standing up causing me to walk quickly. It wasn't until Gramps went back and saw the tracks that I learned I had been followed back by a cougar following the blood dripping from the duck I was carrying. I never left camp alone after that.

The Portland Studio was doing well and Bob and I were asked to move to Canada and open Arthur Murray Dance Studio's in Calgary and Edmonton, Alberta. We went with Jackie and Denise. It was hard to adapt to the bitterly cold winter months lasting for months with snow on the

Jackie, Denise, April & I Williams River

ground. My Mom came up to be with Jackie and Denise while we worked.

In 1954 we became pregnant with our soon to be daughter, April Terri. Soon after April's birth on August 26th, 1955, in Edmonton, Alberta, Bob and I mutually decided to part ways and divorce as our priorities were not aligned and our differences were many.

So again, Mom and I headed back to Portland, this time with Jackie, Denise and April. It was quite a trip back, driving those mountain roads with my mom and the three kids. The kids all were trying to help Momma and Momma trying to help them. We did arrive safely though. Bob remained in Edmonton managing the Edmonton and the Calgary Studios.

After arriving back in Portland we lived with Bob's parents, George and Helen Newberry and his Aunt Helene in their home at 1732 N.E. Wiedler St. in Portland. I again rejoined the Portland studio and was doing well. I was then the West Coast regional manager which included Oregon, Washington, Idaho, Montana, Vancouver, BC and Calgary Alberta. Oh yes, I also had Hawaii in my region. My job was to hold dance clinics at each studio to update and train the instructors in all dances, and also hold sales training sessions on the Katherine Murray manual. After about a year of traveling between the studios in my region, I entered the All American Competition between all the studios. I first won the Portland competition and then the Seattle, then the San Francisco and went on to win New York. Katherine Murray called me the apple cheeked girl from Portland. Part of the prize I had won with the All American Dance Competition, was a trip to Australia to teach the latest dance and sales techniques to the three studios there. Upon completion of my time in Australia, I was given a return ticket to any country I chose.

It was important before leaving on an extended trip, to have my children cared for. Fortunately, grandparents were willing to help. April was loved and cared for by her father's parents the Newberrys,. Jackie and Denise by grandma Gladys, Jack's mother.

Arthur Murray teachers Portland OR

Australia Trip

I spent a week visiting the studio in Hawaii on the way and then went on to Australia. The plane ride to Australia was wonderful, first class with a sleeper, a white curtain pulled across. I screamed though when it was opened by a smiling black face, laughing he informed me it was time to get out for a walk about while we refueled. The whole trip was about 13 hours. Flying over the International Date Line and receiving the certificate was a thrill.

I arrive in Australia 1

Melbourne Australia w/studio manager

When I arrived in Sydney, Australia, I was met with flowers by the manager of the studio, the accountant and the attorney. Australia was a beautiful country with so much to see. The Opera House on the water in Sydney was amazing and the people with their accents were all so nice. The food was wonderful and I learned to eat oysters and lamb. Many beautiful shops and restaurants peppered the city.From Sydney, I moved on to the studio in Melbourne. This city has a long line of history. There are many large ranches and spaces of land occupied by Australia's kangaroos, platypus, and ostriches. This studio was large and had many students. It was said England sent all of their prisoners to Melbourne for so many years.

My next studio in Australia was in Brisbane, a beautiful vacation city with beaches, boats and all kinds of restaurants. It was odd to have summer there when it was winter at home.

My time with the studios in Australia was spent training the instructors in new dance steps such as the west coast swing and teaching interview techniques. I had developed successful sales close for our lifetime membership offer so was also able to teach this. Our student's course always included a weekly party so a good time was had by all. At the conclusion of my three weeks I did an exhibition dance for the three studios attended by the instructors and students alike and spoke of Arthur and Katherine Murray and thanked them all on their behalf. This concluded my working time in Australia and I was off next to see the many exciting Countries.

My first stop after leaving Australia out of Durban was Hong Kong. It was filled with interesting people who spoke different languages and I drew pictures on my sketch pad to remember them. Hong Kong was so beautiful with Sam Pans filling the river that some people lived in their whole lives. I stayed at The Great Eastern Hotel in Kowloon, which was just across the river by ferry, from Hong Kong. Hong Kong was so busy and bustling with streets filled with people and shops and stands. You could buy jewelry or have clothes made to order, all at fantastic savings.

I bought an emerald ring and some clothes. At the hotel, I had

met a nice guy at the bar who was in Hong Kong on business. He invited me to dinner, the hotel had said not to go out that night because some locals were engaged in what they called 'double ten night', involving some shooting but my friend said he knew a great restaurant so we went anyway with no incident. I loved Hong Kong and enjoyed riding the ferry across the river and I rode the trolley up to the Peak for an accelerating and fabulous view. When I checked out of the hotel, they used Abacus beads to total my bill.

My next stop was in Bangkok, Thailand. Arriving in Bangkok was an experience I will never forget. My hotel was on the river in a very pretty area that was mostly all open because it was so hot and no air, just fans. There were many armed guards at the hotel so I felt for the most part safe. I was taken by rickshaw to view the gardens, the palaces and the market place. The market place was very busy and sold handmade items of clothes and jewelry. It was sad though to see the children in the streets. Many of them deformed by their own parents so they could go out on the streets to beg for "buckshee mam". The golden Buddha's were outstanding, decorated with jewels of emeralds and diamonds, each one more beautiful than the last. I also saw a j Ali match that the man that

Hong Kong Harbor

met me at the airport took me to see. It seemed that this was a sport that they excelled in.

Next on was Turkey, when I arrived at the airport I thought they must be at war here because there were soldiers everywhere and people being questioned. I gave them all my papers and identification and walked through the line. It turned out that there was a big shot that just landed in a big plane there so they were making sure everything was secure. I took a cab to my hotel as no one was there to greet me. The hotel was packed and I tried to check in but was told the hotel was full until tomorrow.

Well, now where do I go? They suggested a small hotel so I first ate in the crowded hotel dining room, then set out to find this other hotel. It was on a small dark alley and down some stairs, the person at the front counter was a guy who said he was from the States and gave me a room. The room was about 8 by 10 with nothing in it but a twin bed and a chair. When I looked at the bed, it was crawling with bugs so I sat up all night awake in the chair. The next morning I returned to my beautiful hotel and checked in. The room there was very nice and after resting awhile I took a tour bus to see the main sights. When the driver informed us that we had crossed into Istanbul, I made a remark that this used to be called Constantinople, he said, "Oh, you must know your history." Going back to the airport to leave, the airport was not as chaotic as when I came but there were still a lot of armed guards around. I was happy to get on the plane and leave.

Next, I arrived in Calcutta, India. On the way to the hotel, there were Burmese cows wondering around everywhere. They explained to me that cows are considered sacred there and are catered to. After checking into the hotel, the porter carried my bags to my room then promptly sat cross legged in front of my room. He said he does this to guard from  thieves. A guide took me to the markets that again were crowded with people who were begging and selling anything from food to jewelry. This is where I bought the twin star sapphire ring I later gave to April. Later that evening, I received an invitation from a Maharajah and his Maharani, one of many princes, to have dinner with them. It was a beautiful restaurant with Indian food and music. There were several people in our party and the conversation was interesting. During the conversation, they said they were planning a tiger hunt and would I care to join them? I politely declined but said it sounded exciting. I awoke the next day to a loud crying and flapping of wings of large black birds. I ran to the window to see two men pulling a cart, with sing song hollering and these noisy black birds following along. Later I was told that the birds follow the death carts that pick up the people who had died in the streets during the night. Then I was off to travel again, this time to Rome, Italy.

To visit Rome is to visit all the most cosmopolitan cities in the world rolled into one. The Vatican is an amazing sight, sitting on St. Peters Square. I was not Catholic at that time but made a special effort to buy a round lace scarf to cover my head and visit the Sistine Chapel. It was the most amazing and beautiful site inside with all the famous artist paintings. Michelangelo's painting on the ceiling was beyond words and had taken him years to complete. When he was asked when his work would be finished, he would reply, "I will make a finish when I am finished and not before". I was able to see some of the famous statues, the outstanding colleges and walk across the bridge to the left bank where the famous artists painted their pictures. Though the markets there had all manner of goods, Italy is best known for its leather purses and shoes, the best in the World. The people in Rome all seemed joyful and there were little green urinals that people used right on the street. I also saw some of the wine valleys where some of the famous wines come from. It was a feeling of peace and contentment and though I could not see all of Rome in the few days I had, I knew I would someday be back. I had a wonderful time in Rome and was now headed for London, England, my last stop.

The manager of the London Arthur Murray studio met me at the airport and took me to my hotel not far from the studio. I was given a wonderful tour around London and saw a play but mostly stayed at the studio. The English dancing was more advanced than ours so I attended sessions and learned from them. What I brought for them was the sales program for enlisting life time memberships and other interview techniques. I enjoyed myself in London but was also glad it was my last stop on my wonderful World tour. It had all been so amazing and I had seen and done so much but I looked forward to getting back to my home, my children, my work and a place where I knew the customs and the language.

I had one more stop on my way to Portland, and that was in Florida where my mother, recovering from cancer surgery, had been staying with her sister, my Aunt Lillian. I took a plane straight from London to Miami and spent Thanksgiving with Mom telling her all about my adventures. My stories were fun to tell and it was great to see mom looking good.

At last I was headed home. There is no greater anticipation and feeling of love than returning home to my children. On returning home, I could see how each of the children had grown and they each had their own stories to share with me. One that Denise told was of climbing a tree and coming nose to nose with a porcupine causing her to fall out of the tree, she was such a tomboy. Another was while she and Jack were out playing and sliding down a hill, encountered a hornet's nest and were both stung so bad that Gladys soaked them both in a bath of baking soda for hours. April was still too young at this time but I know she had enjoyed herself with Nana, Granddad and Aunt Lean.

Bob had agreed in our divorce to co-sign for me to buy a house in Portland, as I wanted a home for myself and the children. So, after I returned from my trip, Bob came down from Edmonton to co-sign on my loan and I bought my first home at 3236 N.E. Everett St. in Laurelhurst neighborhood in Portland, Oregon.

The house was a lovely 3 bedroom home with a large backyard and it was in a beautiful, family neighborhood called Laurelhurst, close to schools, church and family. The kids loved the house and the neighborhood, quickly making friends that have remained friends for life. I was again working at the studio in Portland and making a good living.

The kids while on summer vacation and some weekends still spent time with their grandparents. Aunt Lean was also so good about coming and staying at the house when I needed her to. Mostly, we got along fine with a nanny/housekeeper 'Mrs. Mayberry', who was there to watch the children after school.

On Saturdays, I would drive them to swim lessons at Reed College in my pink mustang convertible. We were usually running late and in a hurry so as we drove over the many bumps in the road along the way, the girls would fly up in their seats and we would all laugh and laugh. We also enjoyed going to Rooster Rock on the weekends to play and swim. Though it wasn't their favorite thing to do, the girls also took piano lessons and performed in many recitals. In no time at all, the piano was covered with head statues of composers, given to the students to acknowledge their accomplishments. Jack, who had remained living with Gladys and Gramps was in the school band and marched in the Rose Parade.

The girls loved animals and at one time we had a dog, a rabbit, a hamster and turtles. One time the hamster got loose and Denise stayed up all night in the basement sitting next to a trap she had made. It worked and she caught the hamster.

April was about four during this time and was the first to get the chicken pox. She had a doll named Suzie, that she still has, and she gave Suzie the chicken pox too with indelible ink. We had one neighbor, Mrs. Maxwell who was always shooting at our dog Bo-Bo with a bee-bee gun when he got in her garden and whose Son Billy stabbed one of the neighbor kids with a pitchfork. Our other neighbors were the Nolk's, Doug was the editor of the Oregonian. The girl's best friends were Chris and Bobby Ferris whose father had a travel agency and who later visited us in Baltimore. Other friends were the McCauley's who had five girls and the Bells who lived on the corner. Laurelhurst neighborhood, close to Laurelhurst Park, was the perfect neighborhood for the girls growing up.

The decade of the 50's, became known as The Boom Decade. It was so called for the boom of the economy as well as the Baby Boom created by the soldiers returning home following World War II. This population boom created a need of new home construction which created new jobs and the strength of the nation following the end of World War II.

Dwight D. Eisenhower was nominated President in 1953 and remained in office for two terms to 1961. The Cold War, started in the 50's, a standoff of sorts, as a result of the Soviet East and the Capitalist West both having the power and technology for a Nuclear Holocaust. Fortunately both sides realized this was not the answer.

The 1950's started the Rock & Roll Era when radio stations began playing the music of what was to become the Rock & Roll greats of Elvis Presley, Jerry Lee Lewis and Buddy Holly. This was also the era of the famous crooners like Frank Sinatra, Perry Como and Nat King Cole.

Baseball continued as the most popular sport in the 50's and New York teams like the Yankees, The Giants and The Dodgers ruled the 50's.

Disneyland was opened by Walt Disney in 1955 and became the coveted travel destination by old and young alike.

I cannot fly, or can I?

Walking on the beach, I feel so free.

Birds watching, with twinkling eye,

A soft breeze in the light blue sky.

It's then I know, I understand,

God's footprints there in the sand.

My life is here, but not to stay,

But I will always be here, with the birds and sea

And my soul will fly, and I will be free.

Seychelles

1960's

The 1950's had flown by and we entered the 60's. The 1960's proved to be a decade like no other. President John F. Kennedy was elected as President in 1961 to replace President Eisenhower. He remained in office until that fateful day of November 22nd in 1963 when he was assassinated in Dallas Texas by Lee Harvey Oswald. He was a much beloved President and the Nation was in mourning. It was J.F.K. who said, "Let us ask, not what our country can do for us, but what we can do for our country." He was replaced by Lyndon B. Johnson who was quickly sworn in as President on board Air Force One following the death of President Kennedy. Johnson remained in office until 1969.

The 60's saw America's involvement in the Vietnam War. A war lasting from 1959 to 1975 was not a World War, but one that America entered into to support South Vietnam's battle against the North Vietnam communist allies. We lost many a soldier to this conflict and are still, to this day, seeing the ramifications of it to our Vietnam veterans. It ended in 1975 with no clear victories.

The early 60's were the era of the mini skirt worn with leather boots and men wearing paisley shirts and velvet pants. The later part of the 60's brought in the hippy era with psychedelic clothes of bright colors and men wearing their hair long and women in long jean skirts. This era was mainly brought in by college kids who held demonstrations to protest their views on the Vietnam War and other ills in society in general.

The 60's were also a time of huge advances in space exploration with Apollo missions landing Neil Armstrong and Buzz Aldrin Jr. on the moon. It was Neil Armstrong who announced to Nasa and the world after being the first man to land and walk on the moon, "That's one small step for man, one giant leap for mankind."

The first Super Bowl was played in 1967 between Vince Lombardi's Green Bay Packers and the Kansas City Chiefs. The game was won by Green Bay, 35 to 11 and the Super Bowl and football became an American tradition.

In 1960, I met the man who was to be my lifelong love, Jerry Seitz. I would sometimes stop after work at The Sandy Hut bar for a drink to unwind on my way home from work. It was one of these times that my friend, the bartender there, Dave told me he had a friend he wanted to introduce me to, telling me this guy is a lot of fun and just a great guy. So he introduced me to Jerry. Though I had been dating a Doctor at the time, he didn't stand a chance against Jerry. I agreed to go with Jerry to a Hockey game the next day and after that he would come by the Studio to pick me up for lunch or dinner every day.

After jerry and I were married, it seemed that he enjoyed playing golf on weekends and whenever he had time off work, so that told me, *hey, I had better learn this game to join in the fun.* Jerry was happy to teach me to play golf, bought me some clubs, and we went to play on Glendaver Golf Course. It was a great course near the Columbia river. I started to practice and played with Nancy. She and Fred Allen were our fun great friends then.

One day, playing with Nancy, I teed off on a par three, was surprised that the ball rolled on the green and into the hole. I said, "Oh great. I don't have to putt." Nancy said, "yes. You had a hole in one." I forgot to tell Jerry for a long time because it didn't seem like a big deal, not knowing the rules.

Jerry was great with the girls and they loved him. After about a year of dating, Jerry asked me to marry him in his typical Jerry like way, by asking me "How much are you paying for this house and all anyway? " I told him and he said," I think I can manage that so do you want to get married?" I told him yes and then he told me he loved me and said," you will never need to worry, I will always take care of you for the rest of your life" and he has.

Jerry and I were married at our home in Laurelhurst on May 27th, 1961 and I remember the funny little preacher, wearing a sear-sucker suit who enjoyed too much celebration at the reception following. The wedding was attended by our families and friends including the kids and all their neighborhood friends running through the house. We had a small reception with lots of food and wine. It was a joyous occasion.

Jerry's mother and father, Constance and Ike Seitz lived in Bradford Pennsylvania. In the years to follow we were able to visit them at their home and have them visit us in our various locations. Jerry also has two wonderful older sisters, Hope Ann who was married to Duane Chapin and Toni Sonia Irene who is married to Mike Oleyar. It was nice to be so welcomed into Jerry's family who were now also my family.

We left for our honeymoon at the beach right after because Jerry had the long Memorial Day weekend off. We stayed in Depot Bay in a little hotel right by the ocean. It had a beautiful pool and a restaurant that introduced us to our first Monte Cristo sandwich and the small Olympic oysters. We spent one day going out deep sea fishing, the ocean was so rough that I got so sea sick it was my last time out on a boat of that sort. We had a nice honeymoon and soon settled in as a family.

Jerry and I were married again at The All Saints Catholic church the following May 27th after I completed catechism classes to become a member of the Catholic faith through baptism and confirmation. Jerry was raised Catholic and his faith was important to him. I choose to do this so we could be remarried in the Catholic Church and it was important to both Jerry and I to raise our family in the catholic faith. Both Denise and April also attended Catechism Classes and they, were baptized in the All Saints Church.

In 1962 The Columbus Day Storm hit Portland. It was the worst storm to hit the west coast before or since. Jerry and I had gone for dinner that night on the River Queen boat which was docked on the Willamette River. We didn't know that the storm was coming or how bad it was to be. The anchor broke from the pier and we needed to get off the boat before it was taken by the river. The girls were staying at Nana's house and had an adventure themselves with the old house rocking back and forth. When we all had returned to our home on Everett St., we saw where trees had fallen, cars and houses had been crushed and of-course power was out for a number of days. We were fortunate to not suffer any casualties and made it into fun, cooking over the fire in the living room fireplace and sleeping in sleeping bags in front of the fire.

One day, following a golf game up at Welch's, Jerry arrived home with a baby lamb. The girls were so excited and named him Candy Lamb. Our neighbor Mr. Nolk's informed us that "farm animals" were not allowed in the city" to which Jerry replied, "oh, that's our sheep dog". We fed the lamb with a baby bottle and he followed the girls everywhere like a dog. At that time we had also accumulated a rabbit, named Easter bunny, who we would tie to the willow tree in our backyard and he would go in a circle trimming the branches to the same length all around. We also had two ducks, Arthur and Marion who awoke us as well as our other neighbor, Mrs. Maxwell up promptly at 6:00 am each morning. Though the girls loved having their own petting zoo, we did have to eventually provide Candy Lamb a home at the Zoo and Arthur and Marion, the ducks, homes in the lake at Laurelhurst Park.

Our biggest surprise came toward the end of 62' when we learned we were to have a child. Our son, Stephen Gerhardt Seitz was born in the morning of August, 2nd, 1963 in Portland. We had waited to find out the sex of our baby and Jerry was so thrilled to have a Son. He was such a happy and healthy child who stole all our hearts from the moment we saw him. Connie, Jerry's mother came out to Portland from Bradford, New York and helped with the baby and the girls.

Another adventure we shared, after Steve was born, was when President J.F. K. was assassinated in November of 1963. The nation had closed down in mourning and Jerry decided it would be a good time for us to take the girls for a trip to Disneyland in Los Angeles. So, we hopped in the car and drove all night. The only casualty on that trip was when we hit a deer on the highway. He got up and ran away and Jerry said "Did you see that "big billiard" and we joked about it ever since. We had a great time at Disneyland, Knott's Berry Farm and the Las Angeles zoo. The girls enjoyed getting the hotel manager up at the crack of dawn for their free donuts and orange juice as advertised. One day as we sat by the pool playing Gin Rummy Jerry got upset that I kept winning and threw me in the pool. It was a fun trip for all of us and one the girls will never forget.

We loved to go to the beach on weekends or up to a cabin at Welch's on Mt. Hood. One trip down to the beach, we took our camping stuff and barbeque for food, drove out on the sand, found a place surrounded by tall cliffs, set up a tent for the girls, got out our wine and commenced to watch the sun go down while we fixed dinner. The thing we hadn't counted on was the tide coming in. It came in so fast, it blocked our exit from how we came in. We blocked the wheels of the car with logs, all the while Jerry wondering how he would explain the company car floating out to the sea. We were lucky and the tide stopped just short of the cliffs and the car so we spent the night laughing about it. In the morning, some people came along and we were able to push the car over the sand and leave. We always thought of what could have been.

In 1964 Jerry was offered a promotion with Carborundum Company and we were transferred from Portland to Baltimore, Maryland. It was hard to leave family and friends in Portland but we soon settled in and made a home for ourselves in Baltimore.

We sold my house in Laurelhurst Park, Portland in 1964. This was a big promotion for Jerry. Steve was only one-year-old. The girls, Denny and April, were not looking forward to moving so far away from everything and everyone they grew up with, but we promised they could come back for a visit soon. We also invited their friends to come visit us there. We decided to sell our van that we had enjoyed so much going to Mt. Hood overnights. Steve slept through the whole night first time, in his sleeping bag. We drove to the world fair in New York and visited Toni and Mike in Syracuse and Jerry's parents, Connie and Ike. We camped out along the trip. One night, the girls had their sleeping bags outside when a storm came so fast they were drenched. We stopped in the little towns along the way, found the public swimming pool, and were able to relax and have fun while getting clean. The day we went to the World's Fair, pushing Steve in his carriage, we were all there, but could not understand why Jerry was not happy. Well, no one remembered it was Jerry's birthday. We all thought it was the next day. We made up for it later.

While living in Baltimore, we got our dog, Fritz, he was a Dachshund and soon became a loved member of our family. Steve was about two when we got Fritz and was still in diapers, so when he would have a dirty diaper, he would say 'Free did it', as he called Fritz at that time.

Playing golf was my main hobby outlet. I joined a small club and played with our friends. Lois Crouse and husband Don Crouse. They were so into catching crabs and eating them outside on paper tablecloths. We went on several golf trips with them. They were both pilots and flew their plane to our condo in Daytona. Loise came in and said the weather was so bad with, and with Don not feeling well, she had to fly all the way. So she walked n and said, "Give me a double, Dar," which I did in a hurry. They also flew down from Baltimore to Jerry's 60th birthday party at St. Ives.

We lived in Baltimore at Jan Vale Road. Lois and I had many golf games together. I remember pulling the golf cart up hills and playing when I was eight months pregnant with Stace. We were friends for many years until lois developed lung cancer and passed away. It was very sad to lose her.

We had a home built in Randallstown, Maryland and it was about a year before we were able to move into it but it was so exciting to have our new home on Janvale Road. The neighborhood was great with lots of kids. We hadn't realized until after we moved in that it was a predominately Jewish neighborhood but that didn't matter and all the neighbors were friendly with us. They enjoyed visiting our home at Christmas since we were the only family on the block that decorated their home with lights and had a Christmas tree.

Over one such Christmas, I was as big as a house, as we were expecting again. Margaret Stace Seitz was born in the morning on February 3rd, 1966. Stace's birth was the most exciting of my childbirths as we had had a snow storm in Baltimore and the roads were blocked as I approached the due date. Our neighbor, Mrs. Lieberman, who was a nurse, told me she could help deliver the baby if I went into labor but fortunately Jerry and Denise got our driveway dug out and we had our builder come in with a plow to shovel out our street so we could get out to the hospital. It was an exciting time but we got to the hospital and our beautiful, curly haired, baby girl was born. Stace's first name, Margaret is after her grandmother, my mother. Stace was baptized in Baltimore and her Aunt Toni (God Mother) and Uncle Mike came.

We had an above ground pool in the backyard of our home in Baltimore. It was considered the neighborhood pool and the kids spent hours on hours in the pool with their friends. Jerry had some help with the digging out for the pool when one evening we had gone to a movie and Denise who was not supposed to have friends over when we were out, fell asleep with her friend Eddy on the couch downstairs. When we opened the front door on arriving home, we heard a huge crash, we ran downstairs to find that Eddy, on hearing the front door open jumped up and ran right through the sliding glass door. After making sure he was alright, Jerry asked him "Who do you think you are, the Great Houdini, performing your great escape?" Well, it was agreed that in compensation of our glass door, Eddy would arrive bright and early the next morning and help Jerry with the digging out for our pool, which he did and I think even brought some other friends with him to help.

Martin Luther King became a well-known advocate of equal rights in the 60's with a strong voice and a non-violent approach to promote rights and equality for blacks. He was assassinated in 1968 by James Earl Ray but was instrumental in bringing about The Civil Rights Act of 1964.

The Beatles, who had started out in England became popular in the States in the 60's. After appearing on the Ed Sullivan show with their hit single, "I want to hold your hand", they took off as the most popular performing group of all time. Denise and April went to the stadium to see the Beatles perform. They were so excited to get tickets and looked so forward to the event. There was a lot of unrest in downtown Baltimore at the time and when they came out of the concert, there was a race riot going on. Jerry drove right through it and grabbed the girls in the car. Fortunately, they all got out.

While Denise was in high school, The Beatles hit the scene in a big way and April and Denise went to see their first US performance in Washington, DC at the convention center. It was really a thrill for her to go. Denise graduated from high school from Woodlawn High in Baltimore in 1970 and then, anxious to travel, drove her new Volkswagen Beatle across country, first to Portland and then up to Edmonton, Alberta for a short while. It was there while in Canada that she met and married Alan Kegan.

1970's

The 1970's were now upon us and we were to see three Presidents in this one decade. Richard Nixon had been elected President in 1969 and was forced by threat of impeachment to resign in 1974 when the Watergate scandal came about. The Watergate scandal was the break-in to the Democratic national Committee Headquarters facilitated by the Republican Party's John Mitchell who was Nixon's former Attorney General. Gerald Ford replaced Nixon as President in 1974 and though Nixon was never convicted for his involvement in the scandal, President Ford pardoned him for any offences that he may have perpetrated against the United States. Ford remained in office until 1977 when Jimmy Carter was elected President and remained in office until 1981.

The 1970's remained a time of cultural change with slogans of "Make Love, Not War" and "Flower Power" stated a view of peace not violence in regards to the Vietnam War and college demonstrations where some had turned violent. "Have a nice day" with the smiley face became a common phrase and a know icon. Sit-ins became the new demonstration and movements originated in San Francisco spread across America.

The age of Rock and Roll had progressed to groupls like the Rolling Stones, Jimi Hendricks, Led Zeppelin and others. The famous Woodstock concert that had been held on a farm outside of a town in New York in 1969 was billed as '3 days of peace and rock and roll' and was attended by 500,000. Mick Jagger of the Rolling Stones claimed Woodstock to be the concert that changed the history of rock and roll.

The first personal use computers were starting to emerge and from that technology came the first video games as well as calculators.

In 1970 Jerry was promoted again within The Carborundum Company and we were transferred from Baltimore, Maryland to Lenoir, North Carolina. North Carolina is a beautiful State with lots of green trees, flowers and Mountains. Lenoir is a smaller town, best known for its furniture factories.

We built a house right on the golf course of The Lenoir Golf and Country Club. The kids could go swimming and order lunch then sign the check for it and thought that was pretty high cotton. Steve had learned to play golf in Baltimore and had won his first tournament at age four. I still have the news clipping. He continued playing golf in Lenoir and headed out about every day after school with a golf bag over his shoulder.

In Lenoir, North Carolina, we built a house on a golf course overlooking the second hole. We joined the Cedar Rock Country Club and played a lot of couple's golf. It was a beautiful mountain course. Stace and Steve loved it. The swimming pool they enjoyed also couls sign ticket for lunch with an occasional friend. Steve was really into golf after having learned to play with dad and I at the Baltimore course.

Jimmy Flattery had a children's clinic. He taught a large group of young children. We signed Steve up to play when he was four-years-old and he won the tournament at four-and-a-half.

We enjoyed trips around North Carolina, like up to Boone, a neat little mountain town where we discovered a little restaurant with fabulous home style cooking that we liked to go on Sundays after church.

We attended the Catholic Church there in Lenoir, but as most of the population was Baptist, it was a small congregation of about 100 parishioners and it took all of us pitching in to keep the church up. We would have Father Connelly over for dinner, he was such a good hearted person with a smile for everyone. Jerry had once loaned him his golf cart but was not happy another time when he was headed out to play golf and found that Father Connelly had taken the one time loan as an open invitation to use it. Anyway, we had a lot of fun with the church and Father Connelly. One time, I coordinated a fashion show at our country club to benefit the church, I had a lot of fun doing it and raised quite a bit for our church as well. There was a newspaper picture and article covering the affair.

Another adventure was the day we decided we would go berry picking so I could make fresh blackberry pies. Stacy and Steve got buckets and off we went to fill out buckets with berries. It wasn't until after we got home that we discovered that we were each not only scratched up but covered with ticks. We all had to soak in baths of vinegar to get them off but we sure enjoyed that fresh baked blackberry pie with ice cream. It was a lesson learned when venturing out in the bushes of North Carolina.

In the 70's, after graduating high school, Denise and April both moved back to Portland, Oregon. Jack had always remained in Oregon and married Marcia while we were still in Baltimore. They had three children, my grandchildren, Tammy, Jill and Mike. Jack had a career as a fire fighter, working his way up through the ranks all the way to his retirement. I have always been so proud of him and his family and just had always wished we lived closer together but could well understand his desire to live and raise his family in as beautiful a home as Oregon. He built his home in Oregon City, Oregon, and lives in Oregon still.

Well, we were moving up in the world once again, this time with a transfer to Atlanta, Georgia. I had developed a bad back prior to this move and had to lie in the back seat of the car for the trip down to Atlanta but when we arrived, I thought we were in wonderland. It was spring time in Georgia and all the azaleas and dogwoods were in bloom and everywhere I looked was green and the flowers were beautiful. I loved it on sight.

We found a nice house in the suburbs of Marietta on the golf course of Indian Hills Country Club and immediately settled in and felt at home. We joined the Indian Hills Country Club there and soon made lifelong friends. Steve and Stace also made friends and were involved in their school and activities.

When we first moved to Atlanta, it was spring, with all the flowers in bloom. Azaleas, Dogwood, everything looked like a fairyland. I loved it. We lived in a golf community, Indian Hills Country Club. The club and the golf course were so beautiful. I played almost every day and become more competitive. This is where I won many tournaments including the club championship. We formed so many of our forever friends here.

Nancy and Ken Carlson, Joyce and Bert Lemieux, and I can't name more or I would be leaving out someone.

It wasn't long though before Jerry was again promoted to East Coast Regional Manager and asked to move to Buffalo, New York which was close to the headquarters of Carborundum Company, which was in Niagara Falls, New York. So, we were off again. Though we found a gorgeous home there in a beautiful suburb of Buffalo, we couldn't adapt to the winters. It was so cold, for so many months and with so much snow.

My main activity while in Buffalo was playing Bridge with the other ladies from the club as so much of the year was too cold for golf. The Country Club in Buffalo was rather backward, it had rules that prohibited women from walking through the main club area or having free rein of the club the same as the men. Well, this didn't go over real big with me.

While we were watching the Masters Golf Tournament, which was taking place in Georgia, and seeing all the sun and green that Jerry and I agreed that we needed to move back to Georgia. Jerry was able to convince his work that he could manage the East Coast Region from Georgia so, we once again packed up and moved back to Marietta, Georgia, to where we all considered, by that time, to be our home.

Our boat dock is a relaxing, fun area on the river. It holds our 26 foot Sea Ray, an open boat that all the family has enjoyed on many outings up and down the river.

1980's

In the 80's we moved back to our same Indian Hills neighborhood and the kids quickly reacquainted with their friends, as we did with ours and we were back in the swing of things again, literally. Steve and Stace both finished high school in Georgia and attended a year at the University of Georgia. It was at the Indian Hills Country Club that I won the Ladies Club Golf Championship as well as other golf tournaments.

We had previously bought a shared interest in a Condo in Daytona Beach, Florida with Hope and Duane but had sold it when we transferred to Buffalo. We and the kids missed having our Condo down on the beach so much that we bought our brand new Condo down in Daytona. Seychelles is located right on a private beach, just south of Daytona downtown with 2 bedrooms and a sensational view of ocean and river from the 13th floor. We have all taken every opportunity to go down to the Condo and much time was spent and memories made, playing on the beach, relaxing in the Condo and going out to eat at our favorite spots on the docks.

Steve after completing a year at the University of Georgia chose to enlist in the Air Force and trained to become an air traffic controller. He had been dating Teresa for some time by then and they were married before he was stationed in England. Steve was named the Air Force, Air Traffic Controller of the year while in England and continued to play golf on the Air Force team. It was in England that Steve and Teresa had their first child, my granddaughter, Vanessa.

Stace attended the Atlanta Art Institute at the University of Georgia and pursued her interest in art and advertising. She later met and married Mike Tillman, her children's father. They had their first child, my grandson, Zach in Atlanta the opening night of the 1996 Olympics. Jerry and I had tickets to attend the Olympics but Zach took all night to arrive. They then moved to Charlestown, South Carolina where their second child, my granddaughter, Maddux (Maddie) was born in 2000, which makes her a golden dragon for luck.

In 1984, April, who lived in Portland, Oregon, married Michael Baker. They had their first child, my grandson, Ashton in 1985 and then their second child, my granddaughter, Autumn in 1988. It was hard living so far apart and not seeing my grandchildren or being as much a part of their lives as we would have liked to.

Family Thanksgiving at Condo

We have been fortunate to share a lifelong relationship with Hope and Karl, their cousins, Toni and Mike Oleyar's two children. No matter how often or where we moved Hope and Karl remained constants in our lives. Hope and Karl now each have children as well. Hope has her son Justin and Karl, his daughter Ashley.

When Jerry's company, Carborundum Company, was bought out in 1983, Jerry bought some of their inventory, rented a warehouse space and started his own Company, which we named 'Future Abrasives'. Under Jerry's hard work, knowledge and leadership, the Company soon prospered. Steve, after returning from England and completing his enlistment term with the Air Force, joined his Dad at Future Abrasives and learned the business from top to bottom. Steve and Teresa's second child, my grandson, Nicholas was born in Atlanta, Georgia.

As Future Abrasives grew into a solid and successful business, we found a lot in Alpharetta, Georgia at 9 North Drive and had a warehouse/plant built to Jerry's specifications.

We eventually moved from Indian Hills to a home we built in St. Ives Country Club and lived there for about five years, closer to Alpharetta, but still close enough to our friends in Indian Hills.

The 80's were referred to as the New Age or self-help era as people became aware of their diets, the food they ate and jogging came about at this time as well as self-help books becoming popular.

President Regan was President from 1981 to 1989. It was President Regan, who, on a visit to Berlin, Germany, while giving a speech to the people said, "Mr. Gorbachev, tear down this wall". It was later in the 80's that Germany saw The Collapse of the Berlin Wall and the fall of the Soviet Union which constituted the end of the Cold War.

The feminist movement was in full swing, encouraging the equality of women in home, jobs and equal pay. As women gained independence outside of their role of raising their children and keeping the home, a dilemma presented itself to modern women as they became torn between their family and career. Some men saw their roles reversed to the stay at home partner while their wife's worked.

In the 80's, home computers really hit the scene and it was soon that every house had their own personal computer. It was also the decade that we started to see personal use beepers and cellular mobile phones. Video games like Mario Brothers and others became popular with the kids and started the video game craze.

Sports saw the first Baseball strike by the players and though they won the strike, they lost a large fan base. The 1980's in Football was pretty much dominated by quarterback Joe Montana.

1990's

In 1998, after much cajoling, I convinced Jerry that it was time to look toward retirement and we bought our lot to build our retirement home, in Hammock Dunes Country Club, in Florida. We loved the lot, it is on the St. Johns coastal waterway, on a large lot with wonderful Oak trees in the front.

During our last year in Atlanta, for Christmas, I surprised Jerry with his wish for a large dog. Sammy was just a tiny ball of fluff when we first got her but she soon grew into her large paws to become a beautiful golden lab. Well, Sammy entered our lives with much love. She provided constant companionship, staying with Jerry at work, accompanying him on many a road trip, and she always sat in the front passenger seat, with me in the back. Everyone loved Sammy, the kids, when small would fall asleep on her tummy or she would roll the ball to them with her nose. She was always as much a part of our lives and home as any other family. We shared 14 years of love and memories with Sammy and when she left us she knew that she was loved. We will always miss her.

While I supervised the building of our home, Jerry stayed in an apartment in Alpharetta, Georgia, near his work with Sammy and I stayed at our Condo in Daytona Beach, close to where our new home was being built. Jerry and I managed to see each other regularly during this time with him coming down to

Daytona or me going up to Georgia. Jerry sent me flowers about every other week and it was like our second honeymoon. I will always see Sammy, with her smiling face, sitting in the front passenger seat keeping Jerry company, as he made his weekend trips down to Daytona to see me and the progress of our home.

We remained in Georgia until Jerry's retirement in 1999. His retirement party was attended by all his employees as well as friends and family. It was really a tribute to him and how much he was thought of and would be missed. Jerry then turned the reins of Future Abrasives over to Steve who bought out our interest in the Company and is carrying on his father's dream.

In July of 1999, we moved from Atlanta to our beautiful new home at Hammock Dunes, in Palm Coast, Florida. It's here that we have resided since. We have not for a minute regretted our choice of retirement locations. The Country Club here at Hammock Dunes is beautiful, the town of Palm Coast is quaint and we've enjoyed every second spent here at our home. We had a boat dock built on the waterway when we built our home and bought a boat after we moved in, we have enjoyed our boat rides on the river. We have been fortunate to have many of our very good friends move down to the area here as well. It's been our paradise and the longest we have continually lived in one place.

Our time during retirement has been spent traveling, playing golf, getting together with friends and enjoying our family.

2000's

Denise moved to Florida in 2000 and bought a house in Palm Coast, not far from us. She started her own business and enjoys working in her beautiful garden and fixing up her home. She recently battled cancer for two years and we give thanks every day for her recovery.

Stace, with Zach and Maddie also moved down to Palm Coast following her time in Charleston. We couldn't have been happier to have her and the kids just across the river from us. She met her true love, Mike Murphy and they were married on the beach at the condo in Daytona in 2010. Their family now has their home in Jacksonville Florida, close enough to see them often, which we love to do.

Steve, Teresa, Vanessa and Nick have always remained in Georgia. So fortunately, over the years, we have never been too far away from them to be able to go up to visit them and have them come down to visit us. We were greatly saddened by the loss of Teresa, our daughter in-law of 27 years who we lost in 2012 to cancer. Teresa was much loved and will always be remembered and missed.

We have also since our retirement, been able to visit Jack and his family in Oregon as well as April, Michael and Autumn in Corpus Christi, Texas, Colorado Springs, Colorado and

Vancouver, BC. Each of them and their families have also visited us in Florida and enjoyed stays at the Condo in Daytona Beach. Our grandson Ashton enlisted in the Army in 2003 and worked his way up through the ranks for the next seven years. Although we were fiercely proud of him and his service to his country, it was hard having him away and deployed 3 separate times. We prayed for him and missed him. We have been happy to see him on the occasions he has visited us in Florida as he now lives in Texas.

We've had our Condo, Seychelles for over 30 years now and it has given us and our whole family so much joy and so many memories. The grandkids basically all grew up visiting the condo through the years. Many a day has been spent on the beach or in the pool. We have also hosted many momentous occasions there in the penthouse, Thanksgiving dinners, Stace's marriage to Mike Murphy, and Jerry's Birthday party.

Golf has played a significant role in my life. Jerry taught me to play golf after we were first married and it has been an enjoyment of social interaction and fellowship with our friends in the different clubs throughout our lives. I have enjoyed playing golf for over 50 years now and have

won many trophy's, including the Ladies Championship at Indian Hills Country Club, the Senior Club Championship at St. Ives Country Club and a hole in one, on mother's day no less, at Hammock Dunes Country Club. I have enjoyed needling my husband and son that I have them one up. I'm happy to see the

Ladies Golf Association make progress in their prejudice toward women in golf over the last few years. Things really changed when the first women, Condoleezza Rice, was invited to join the Augusta National Country Club. I remember when we belonged to Park Country Club in Buffalo, New York, that women were not allowed to go through the front door of the club but rather needed to enter through the ladies room side door.

We have taken a number of fabulous trips and cruises since our retirement. Some trips we have taken with friends or family and some with just Jerry and I, like our 50th Anniversary trip to Hawaii. We've been to Alaska, Rome, Russia, Ireland, Hawaii, The Bahamas, The Caribbean, Greece and the Panama Canal.

One of the most memorable sites we visited, for me, was visiting what is said to be the home of The Virgin Mother Mary.

It is located on Mt. Koressos, Turkey, translated Mount Nightingale. It was a small house with a garden and a fence around it. The belief is that Mary, the mother of Jesus was taken to this house by St. John following the resurrection and ascension of Jesus and lived there until she died. It had all kinds of notes from people written to Mary tacked on the walls. Seeing this helped me to see Mary as a real person. It gave me chills and filled me with joy.

This collection of stories is just a few of the things that have happened during my life. The most important part of my life is, always has been and always will be my family. I have been blessed to have five wonderful children and the best husband in the world.

Jack, my first child, has always found his way with a steadfast determination and integrity. He has given of himself to his career as a firefighter and also in his role as a father. He has

raised three wonderful grandchildren, Tammy, Jill and Mike.

Denise, my first daughter, has always stood by my side. She has always helped others selflessly, even while battling her own adversities with quiet determination. She has a heart of gold and has contributed to and made a difference through her life to so many others in so many ways.

Next is my gift from God, my sweet, strong, adorable daughter April. How can I thank her for all the love, help and consideration she has given me. She has been a wonderful mother to our grandchildren, Ashton and Autumn.

My son Steve, I cannot say enough about. I am proud to say he is a great man as well as a great father. He has come through heartache and loss and managed to live his life with calm, honest integrity. All the while keeping a sense of humor and knowing what is best for his children, our grandchildren, Vanessa and Nicholas.

And my baby, my Stace. Though in my heart she has always been my beautiful baby girl, she has never let me baby her. She has always known her own way and has always been determined and strong. Stace cares and loves deeply. She protects her children and her loved ones. She is a wonderful mother to our grandchildren, Zach and Maddie Tillman.

My husband Jerry is the pillar of my life and our family. He has always held everything and everyone together with his beliefs in God, in family and a strong conviction to fairness and standing by his word.

I am so proud of each of my grandchildren, each have grown to be exceptional people with outstanding attributes. I couldn't be prouder of them or love each of them more.

Last but certainly not least, I remember my mother. She was born January 19th, 1908 and died April 19th, 1988 at 80 years old. She lived her life to the fullest in her home in Taylorville, Illinois with her faithful companion, Missie. Mother loved all her grandchildren and managed to make trips down to Atlanta to visit us. She loved to make quilts and made one for each grandchild to remember her by. The last she made was for me and I cherish and treasure it. Mothers motto was; Once a task is first begun, never leave it till it's done, if the task be big or small, do it well or not at all. I loved mother with all my heart, admired her for all she was and still miss her so much.

2010's

As I sit here reflecting after my 88th birthday, nearly nine decades after my birth, there are so many times, so many people so much more that I would have liked to have included, but there is only so much space in a small book. It would be great to tell about our golf trips with friends, and that putt that dropped or each of the children's weddings, or the heartache of losing someone dear. We all have stories to tell and I urge you to tell them and to cherish each day.

Believe in yourself, your strengths and your abilities. Be proud and stand tall! Be honest. Love returns love. Always be positive and know you can live life to its fullest. Don't be afraid to grab hold of every opportunity and work to make it happen. You know I love you all and hope you have a wonderful life. God Bless,

Your Mom.

A quick addendum:

My granddaughter, Autumn, who is my daughter April's daughter, married to Nate Shanne, just had a beautiful 8 lb girl. Her name is Ashlyn Schanne and she is my GREAT Granddaughter.

Steve Seitz has announced his intentions to we'd. Jennifer McGrath on June27th 1914. In the invitation he said "it's early Friday evening and a warm Caribbean wind is gently caressing nearby palms causing them to whisper their quiet song of love to anyone who may be listening. Out at sea, the aging sun takes one last breath of the day as it strains to kiss the deep blue ocean once again."

And so life goes on…

Make life your dance!

www.ingramcontent.com/pod-product-compliance
Lightning Source LLC
Chambersburg PA
CBHW060043230426
43661CB00004B/635